Delaware Statutory Trust (DST) Properties – An Introduction to DST Properties for 1031 Exchange Investors

By: Dwight Kay,
Founder and CEO of Kay Properties and Investments, LLC

This book is dedicated to my little brother,
Jesse John Payne Kay.
Thanks for believing in me, I love you and I can't wait to
see you in the blink of an eye...

Foreword:

Thank you very much for purchasing this book on 1031 exchange Delaware Statutory Trust (DST 1031) properties. This book is meant to serve as an introduction for you the reader to DST 1031 properties as you begin to explore if they are the right fit for your upcoming 1031 exchange.

I decided to write this book because there is no other published volume available to 1031 exchange investors on DST properties that I am aware of. I believe that education has been one of the reasons for the growth of my company, Kay Properties and Investments LLC, over the years and I hope that you enjoy learning more about this subject matter in an easy-to-read, as non-technical as possible format.

I also invite you to receive a wealth of additional information on DST 1031 properties for free by registering at my website kpi1031.com. You will receive access to a large amount of valuable content, such as a currently available DST 1031 property menu, white papers, infographics and educational videos.

Lastly, if you have further questions and want more in-depth details on your options with DST 1031 properties, feel free to email me at dwightkay@kpi1031.com.
I hope you enjoy this book!

Best Regards,

-- Dwight Kay

Looking for more insight on DST properties? Attend one of our free upcoming educational conference calls by registering at kpi1031.com/register.

Table of Contents

Risks and Disclosures:

This book is not intended to be an exhaustive document and contains general information on DST 1031 properties. This information, including the numbers, statistics and examples herein, is general in nature, approximate and intended for educational purposes only.

Please remember that this book is not intended to provide any tax or legal advice to you. We highly encourage all readers of this book to speak with their CPA and attorney prior to considering an investment in a DST 1031 property for all tax and legal advice. We also encourage you to speak with your CPA and attorney to determine if an investment in DST 1031 properties may be suitable for your particular circumstances.

There are risks associated with investing in DST 1031 properties, including, but not limited to, that you could lose your entire principal amount invested. We have outlined additional risk factors in Chapter 3. We also encourage you to read each prospective DST 1031 property's full offering materials and Private Placement Memorandum (PPM) prior to investing, paying careful attention to the risk section.

Chapter 1:
DST 1031 Properties – The Basics

Chapter 1:
DST 1031 Properties – The Basics

A Delaware Statutory Trust (DST) is an entity that is used to hold title to investment real estate. In some ways, this is similar to how a Limited Liability Company (LLC) can hold title to real estate; however, unlike an LLC, a DST 1031 property will qualify as "like kind" exchange replacement property for a 1031 exchange. This qualification as "like kind" property is pursuant to the Internal Revenue Code Section 2004-86.

The DST entity can be used to hold title to most types of real estate; however, a typical DST 1031 property is a triple net (NNN) leased retail or office property or a multifamily apartment community. A NNN leased property is a property whereby the tenant (and not the landlord) is typically responsible for property maintenance costs, insurance premiums and property taxes.

Other types of DST 1031 properties that have been available to investors have included shopping centers, government leased buildings, self-storage facilities, senior living communities, warehouses, distribution facilities, medical office buildings, fast food buildings, pharmacies and grocery stores.

Typically, at any given time, Kay Properties has 10 to 15 DST 1031 properties available to our qualified accredited clients, with a typical minimum investment of $100,000.

The following are hypothetical examples of DST 1031 properties, and actual properties, tenants, lease terms and financing structures may vary greatly. Please note that the names listed below are independent of Kay Properties and Investments and belong to their respective copyright and trademarked companies. Please also note that there are material risks associated with investing in real estate and DST properties, including but not limited to loss of entire principal amount invested. Please review the risk section of the private placement memorandum for any potential DST offering that you are considering, and speak with your CPA and attorney prior to investing.

- A 300-unit class-A multifamily community located in Austin, Texas. The property is 97 percent occupied and financed with a long-term non-recourse loan provided by Fannie Mae.

- A portfolio of four Walgreens throughout the United States that are 100 percent occupied on an absolute-NNN lease by Walgreens corporate.

- An all-cash, debt-free CVS pharmacy on a corporate-backed, long-term 25-year absolute-NNN lease.

- A 15-story office building that is 100 percent occupied as the headquarters of a major Fortune 500 company on a long-term NNN lease.

- A 100 percent occupied, NNN leased BJ's Wholesale Club located in the New York metropolitan area.

- A 478-unit, class-A self-storage facility located in Dallas, Texas.

- A portfolio of 12, 100 percent occupied, single tenant, freestanding net lease properties located throughout the country. Tenants include CVS, Walgreens, McDonald's, Tractor Supply Company, Auto Zone, 7 Eleven, Dollar General, Kentucky Fried Chicken (KFC), Taco Bell, Applebee's, Sherwin Williams and KinderCare.

- A 250-unit, class-B plus multifamily apartment community located in Boston, Massachusetts and 95 percent occupied.

- Lastly, a medical office building, 100 percent leased to the University of California, Los Angeles Health System on a 15-year NNN lease.

DST 1031 properties also have various financing ratios to satisfy an investor's exchange requirements of taking on "equal or greater debt," as defined by the Internal Revenue Code Section 1031. However, some DST 1031 properties are offered all-cash, debt-free in order to mitigate the risk of using financing when purchasing real estate.

The financing used on DST 1031 properties is typically non-recourse to the investor. Non-recourse financing is typically defined as financing whereby the lender's only remedy in the case of a default is the subject property itself.

The lender is not able to pursue the investor's other assets beyond the subject property. So, investors could lose their entire principal amount invested in the property in the case of a major tenant bankruptcy, market-wide recession or depression, but their other assets would be protected from a lender.

The non-recourse financing used on DST 1031 properties is typically long-term (usually seven to 20 years) and already locked and in place with the lender. This can greatly help to reduce 1031 exchange closing risk for investors that must be able to identify a property within their 45-day identification period that they know that are going to be able to close on.

From our observations at Kay Properties, the typical loan to cost of a DST 1031 property ranges between 40-65 percent as of this writing in 2015. A DST 1031 property with a 50 percent loan to cost is a property wherein the investors are putting down half of the required equity or cash amount to purchase the DST property and the lender is providing the other half, in the form of a mortgage.

As an owner of the DST 1031 property, you will typically receive 100 percent of your pro-rata portion of any potential principal pay-down from the loan on the property, thereby potentially building equity in the property. It is important to note that some DST 1031 properties are structured with principal pay-down beginning the first year, others with principal pay-down beginning in year two to five and others that are interest-only financing for the life of the loan.

DST 1031 properties are structured whereby the investors

in the DST receive 100 percent of their pro-rata portion of the potential rental income generated by the property's tenants. DST investors receive 100 percent of their pro-rata portion of any potential net appreciation of the property over the hold period. This is an area that truly differentiates DST 1031 properties from partnerships. With a partnership, the offerings sponsor is typically entitled to a portion of the potential rental income and potential appreciation.

Investors are keenly interested in the fact that when a DST 1031 property is sold, they are free to do another future 1031 exchange into any type of "like kind" replacement property. Typically, our clients at Kay Properties and Investments do further 1031 exchanges into more DST 1031 properties; however, you are free to invest in any other type of "like kind" property that you choose to upon the sale of your DST property.

From our observations at Kay Properties, we see DST 1031 properties, as of this writing in 2015, providing a projected cash-on-cash return of between 5 and 8 percent. The cash-on-cash return is a metric used in real estate to determine return on equity and is commonly referred to as cash flow. The variation in projected cash flows is due to a number of factors such as asset class (commercial properties typically provides a higher projected cash flow than multifamily apartments), location (strong primary markets like New York City and San Francisco typically have lower projected cash flows than smaller secondary or tertiary markets), age of the buildings, years remaining on the primary lease term and strength of the tenant (Are they considered investment-grade by Standard and Poor's or non-investment grade? Is it a public or private company? Does the company have a positive growth outlook or is it a contracting industry?). These are just some of the factors that can influence projected cash flows on DST 1031 properties.

The projected cash flow on DST 1031 properties is a "net" number to DST investors. This means the projected cash flow is "net" of all management fees, debt service payments and property expenses. For example, if an investor invests $1 million into a DST 1031 property with a projected cash flow of 7 percent, the net amount projected to be sent to the investor that year is $70,000. DST 1031 properties' projected cash flow is typically paid to the DST owners on a monthly basis via either ACH direct deposit straight into the investors checking or savings accounts or a physical check (whichever the investor prefers).

It is important to note that cash flow from real estate and DST 1031 properties, as well as past performance, is not guaranteed, as it is a function of the underlying real estate and tenants and their economic performance. Just as with all other types of real estate, projected cash flows could be lower than anticipated. It is very important for you as an investor to believe in the property, its location and its tenants before investing, as well as to review the risk factors of the offering materials in their entirety.

With DST 1031 properties investors are able to utilize depreciation and interest write-offs to partially shelter their projected cash flow from taxes. This allows for tax-advantaged potential rental income to the investor. This is another reason why many of our clients have invested non-1031 exchange discretionary funds into DST 1031 properties, which we will look into further in Chapter 6.

A typical DST 1031 property can be closed on within five business days after submitting subscription documents. DST 1031 properties can be closed on this quickly because typically all of the appraisals, environmental reports, property condition reports, financing, tenant estoppels, etc. have already been completed, as DST 1031 properties are "pre-packaged" for 1031 exchange investors. This is one of the reasons why DST 1031 properties have become very popular with investors that are in their 45-day identification period and close to running the risk of a failed 1031 exchange and a major tax consequence. They like the fact that they can close on DST 1031 properties quickly and complete their 1031 exchange within IRS guidelines.

DST 1031 investors do not receive a K-1 or 1099 at the end of the year for tax purposes. At the end of the year you will receive an operating statement (sometimes referred to as a substitute 1099). This will show your pro-rata portion of the DST properties rental income and expenses.

You will then provide this to your CPA, who will take this information and input it into Schedule E on your tax return, the same as all of your other commercial and rental properties.

DST 1031 properties are only available to accredited investors. An accredited investor (1) is generally defined as an investor with a net worth (assets minus liabilities) of greater than $1 million, exclusive of primary residence. That being said, there are a number of ways that an entity can potentially qualify as an accredited investor, and we encourage all investors to speak with their CPA and attorney before considering a DST 1031 investment to fully ascertain if you and your investment entity (trust, partnership, LLC, etc.) qualify as an accredited investor.

Would you like even further information on DST 1031 properties? Register at kpi1031.com to receive your free PowerPoint presentation on DST 1031 properties with graphs, illustrations and photos designed to help further educate our clients.

(1) http://www.investor.gov/news-alerts/investor-bulletins/investor-bulletin-accredited-investors

Chapter 2:
What Are the Potential Benefits of Exchanging into a DST Property?

Chapter 2:
What Are the Potential Benefits of Exchanging into a DST Property?

There are a number of potential benefits of exchanging into a DST 1031 property. It is important to note that these should be carefully weighed with the potential risks that we will outline in the next chapter. You should also read the risk section of each DST 1031 property's offering materials in detail prior to investing.

Eliminating the day-to-day headaches of property management

Many of our clients are at or near retirement, and they are tired of the hassles that real estate ownership and management often bring. They are tired of the tenants, toilets and trash and are wanting to move away from actively managing properties. The DST 1031 property provides a passive ownership structure, allowing them to enjoy retirement, grandkids, travel and leisure, as well as to focus on other things that they are more passionate about instead of property management headaches.

Tax deferral using the 1031 exchange

Many of our clients have wanted to sell their apartments,

rentals and commercial properties for years but haven't been able to find a property to exchange into and just can't stomach the tax bill after adding up federal capital gains tax, state capital gains tax, depreciation recapture tax and the Medicare surtax. The DST 1031 property solution provides investors an ability to move from an active to a passive role of real estate ownership on a tax-deferred basis.

Increased cash flow potential

Many investors are receiving a lower amount of cash flow on their current properties than they could be, due to their properties having under-market rents, properties that have multiple vacancies and/or that are raw or vacant land sitting idle. DST 1031 exchange properties provide an opportunity for investors to potentially increase their cash flow on their real estate holdings via a tax deferred 1031 exchange.

Portfolio diversification by geography and property types

Often times, 1031 investors are selling a property that comprises a substantial amount of their net worth. They want to reduce their potential risk and instead of buying one property (such as another apartment building) or one NNN building (such as a Walgreens pharmacy or Taco Bell restaurant) they decide that investing into a diversified portfolio of DST 1031 properties with multiple locations, asset classes (property types) and tenants is a better fit for their goals and objectives.

This is similar to how investors tend to invest retirement funds in mutual funds and Exchange Traded Funds (ETFs), as opposed to placing their entire retirement savings into the stock of one particular company. However, it is important to note that there are no assurances that diversification will produce profits or guarantee against loss.

Long-term non-recourse financing locked and in place to satisfy debt replacement requirements of the 1031 exchange

One of the requirements for a 1031 exchange is to take on "equal or greater debt" in the replacement property to what you had in the relinquished property (the property you are selling). In today's lending environment, it is often hard for investors to obtain non-recourse financing at an acceptable interest rate and terms. Due to the DST 1031 properties' sponsors typically having strong lending relationships, they are able to secure non-recourse financing at some of the best terms available in the marketplace. The DST 1031 investors are the direct recipient of these financing terms that they would otherwise often not be able to obtain on their own.

Access to Institutional Grade Real Estate

DST 1031 properties provide access to large, institutional-grade real estate that is often otherwise outside of an individual investor's price point. With the typical minimum investment of $100,000, investors are still able to purchase an ownership interest in large $20 million-plus apartment communities, $5 million-plus pharmacies or $15 million grocery stores, for example. This allows investors access to a level of real estate that they just would not have been able to exchange into before.

That being said, we also have had many clients with very large 1031 exchanges opt to invest in DST 1031 properties because they did not want to place "all their eggs into one basket" by purchasing one single, large investment property.

Unlocking trapped equity

For those investors that have a substantial amount of equity in raw or unimproved land (as well as investors with vacant properties that are not producing any cash flow), the DST 1031 property allows them the opportunity to sell, defer taxes via a 1031 exchange and unlock the trapped equity that they have in their properties. Now this trapped equity is free to produce for the investor potential cash flow on a monthly basis.

Ability to typically close on a DST 1031 property typically within three to five business days of completing and returning subscription documents

This is one of the main reasons why investors in their 45-day identification period "time crunch" often turn to DST properties. They are able to close quickly and complete their exchanges due to the properties being pre-packaged, as opposed to waiting 30, 60 or 90 days to purchase another outside property.

Increased tax efficiency due to depreciation deductions on replacement property

Investors that have owned their apartments and rental properties for longer than 27.5 years and commercial properties for longer than 39 years have fully depreciated the properties, with no more deductions to help shelter the rental income. By purchasing DST 1031 properties that have a greater amount of financing than their relinquished (sold) properties, those investors are creating for themselves a new basis to shelter rental income through. We encourage all investors to speak with their CPA and tax attorney regarding this prior to investing in DST 1031 properties for details regarding their particular situation.

Increased tax efficiency due to interest write-offs

For investors that have fully paid off their properties, the DST 1031 properties with financing in place provide for interest write-offs to help shelter potential cash flows. Many clients in today's environment are looking for a way to increase tax efficiency due to the burdensome tax system in place in the United States. The DST 1031 can help to potentially solve some of these tax problems.

Chapter 3:
What Are the Risks of DST 1031 Properties?

Chapter 3:
What Are the Risks of DST 1031 Properties?

DST 1031 properties are comprised of real estate and contain the same risks that all other forms of real estate entail. The following discussion on risks is meant to be an overview of potential risks and not an exhaustive list. We encourage investors to review the risk section of each potential DST 1031 property's offering materials before investing.

All forms of real estate investing, whether buying homes, duplexes, apartment buildings, commercial properties, including DST 1031 properties, are speculative and involve a high degree of risk. They are considered speculative because there are no guarantees with real estate investing. Investors should be able to bear the complete loss of an investment. All real estate and DST 1031 properties are subject to the risks of increased and ongoing vacancy, tenant bankruptcies, problematic tenants, economic downturns, physical damage, unexpected repairs and maintenance, eminent domain, negative rezoning, blight, environmental damage and liability and overall valuation fluctuations.

Further risks of real estate and DST 1031 properties include (but are not limited to) no guarantees for projected cash flows, no guarantees for projected appreciation, illiquidity, loss of day-to-day management control, interest rate risk and potential loss of entire principal amount invested.

The use of leverage in real estate investments may increase volatility and the overall risk of loss. Furthermore, real estate investments and DST 1031 properties entail fees related to the acquisition, syndication, ongoing management and eventual disposition of the properties. These fees could materially impact the performance of an investment.

Again, please do speak with your CPA and attorney regarding the risks of investing in DST 1031 properties, along with reviewing the entire offering materials, which provide a full discussion of risks.

IRS Guidelines for DST 1031 Compatibility

When the IRS issued the Revenue Ruling 2004-86 (1), it allowed a properly structured DST to qualify as a like kind 1031 exchange replacement property. Along with this Revenue Ruling, the IRS issued seven "deadly sins," as we call them, which placed limitations on the trustee of any DST property.

These limitations are:
1. Once the offering is closed, there can be no future contributions of capital to the Delaware Statutory Trust or DST by either current or new co-investors or beneficiaries.
2. The Trustee of the Delaware Statutory Trust or DST cannot renegotiate the terms of the existing loans, nor

can it borrow any new funds from any other lender or party.
3. The Trustee cannot reinvest the proceeds from the sale of its real estate.
4. The Trustee is limited to making capital expenditures with respect to the property to those for (a) normal repair and maintenance, (b) minor non-structural capital improvements and (c) those required by law.
5. Any liquid cash held in the Delaware Statutory Trust or DST between distribution dates can only be invested in short-term debt obligations.
6. All cash, other than necessary reserves, must be distributed to the co-investors or beneficiaries on a current basis, and
7. The Trustee cannot enter into new leases or renegotiate the current leases.

The seven deadly sins can be problematic for 1031 exchange investors and potentially trigger unforeseen tax consequences to investors. Most sponsors have structured the DST with master leases, allowing them the flexibility to address some of the issues that the seven deadly sins can create. Also, most sponsors will typically use long-term financing that will potentially allow a DST property to be sold prior to the need to either pay off or refinance the loan on the property. However, there are no guarantees that a master lease or long term financing can protect investors from unforeseen tax consequences.

Investors should speak with their CPA and attorney for a full discussion of the implications of the DST structure, including the seven deadly sins, prior to making an investment into any DST offering.

All real estate and DST properties entail fees and costs that investors should review and consider carefully with their CPAs and attorneys prior to making an investment. Fees and costs should be weighed carefully against the potential for tax deferral using a 1031 exchange. All fees and costs are outlined in each offering's Private Placement Memorandum for investors to review and agree to prior to making an investment.

Loan Securitization Risk

Some of the DST 1031 properties are financed with commercial mortgage-backed security (CMBS) financing. This is financing wherein a financial institution will make a loan to a borrower and then package that loan with many other loans in a trust, which is then typically sold to institutional investors looking for income. CMBS financing can pose substantial risks to DST 1031 investors due to the unique structure of CMBS financing and special servicers typically being very aggressive against CMBS borrowers that are in any type of default of the loan provisions. Many institutional buyers of commercial real estate utilize CMBS financing due to the competitiveness of the loan terms and rates offered; however, it is important to note that if an investor is uncomfortable with CMBS financing, he or she should not invest in a DST 1031 property that will be using it. All investors should review with their attorney and CPA the loan details found in the PPM as well as the loan documents provided upon request by the sponsor company regarding any DST 1031 offering.

Again, the risks discussed above are not meant to be an

exhaustive list of risks involved with real estate investments and DST properties. We do encourage investors to read each offering's Private Placement Memorandum (PPM) completely and to pay careful attention to the risk factors section.

(1) http://www.irs.gov/irb/2004-33_IRB/ar07.html

Chapter 4:
Illiquidity and Exit Strategies

Chapter 4:
Illiquidity and Exit Strategies

Two of the questions that often come up from our clients considering a DST 1031 exchange property are 1) How liquid are DST 1031 properties? and 2) What are the exit strategies?

First off, it is important to note first and foremost that DST 1031 properties are real estate, and like all other types of real estate they are inherently illiquid. You are not buying shares of stock listed on a public exchange that you can sell in 10 seconds by logging into your online brokerage account. This is a fractional beneficial interest in a trust that owns a large piece of illiquid real estate. Investors should be able and willing to hold their investment in a DST 1031 property for the full life of the program, which could last for seven to ten years or even longer.

That being said, we have heard of investors selling their DST 1031 interest in a property before. One of the main issues is finding another buyer and agreeing on a price. Typically, if an investor wants to sell their interest in a DST 1031 property, the sponsor will send a letter to all of the other DST investors in the property notifying them that a fellow investor wants to exit their interest in the property.

There is no guarantee that an investor will be able to find another investor that wants to buy his or her DST interest and that they will be able to agree to a price. Therefore, DST 1031 properties again are to be considered illiquid investments and should only be purchased if an investor is able and willing to hold the investment for the full life of the DST offering.

The second question is "What is the exit strategy?" This answer is always unknown until a particular DST actually goes "full cycle." Full cycle is a term used to describe a DST property that is purchased on behalf of investors and then after a period of time is sold on behalf of investors. The following are various exit strategies that could potentially take place; please note that this is not an exhaustive list of potential exit strategies but merely a list of examples for illustration purposes only:

1) A Real Estate Investment Trust (REIT) purchases the DST property.
2) A large institution, such as a pension fund or foreign investor, purchases the DST property.
3) Another real estate company on behalf of their investors purchases the DST property.
4) An ultra-high net worth buyer will purchase the DST property via a 1031 exchange or as an outright purchase.
5) The investors in a DST property are potentially given an option to utilize the Section 721 exchange to exchange into a larger portfolio of properties (such as a REIT) on a tax-deferred basis. This potential exit strategy is examined further in chapter 7.

Chapter 5:
Who Is Who - The Roles of DST Industry Players

Chapter 5:
Who Is Who - The Roles of DST Industry Players

Many investors find it hard to keep the players in the DST 1031 industry straight in their minds. Who is the sponsor, the broker dealer, and the registered representative? This chapter seeks to answer these questions and provide a background for potential DST 1031 investors on "who is who."

DST Real Estate Sponsor Companies

A real estate sponsor company creates the DST 1031 property for investors to be able to invest in. The creation of a DST 1031 property is a very complex process that involves many different facets.

The role of the DST sponsor company is to locate potential properties to be used in a DST 1031 offering. The DST sponsor will typically review and analyze dozens and dozens of potential properties before finding a property that fits.

Once finding a property that potentially fits, the sponsor company begins to run financial models on the property to decide if it will work as an actual DST offering.

The DST sponsor company will from there begin to open up negotiations with the prospective property's seller via a letter of intent, due diligence period and then entering into a Purchase and Sale Agreement.

During due diligence the DST sponsor company will typically order all environmental reports, appraisals and property condition/engineer reports, as well as conduct an analysis of the property's lease and market/sub market.

The DST sponsor will also (if the property is not going to be an all-cash property) begin to arrange and negotiate financing and terms with potential lenders.

From there, the DST sponsor company will begin to market the DST 1031 offering to broker dealers and registered representatives in an effort to raise the required equity to fully fund the offering.

Once the offering is fully funded, the DST sponsor company will typically continue to have an active role with the property and investors, typically as the property asset manager. An asset manager's role is to manage the properties and their tenants from a financial and legal perspective. The asset manager is often considered the manager of the property manager.

Some sponsors will act as the property manager of the DST 1031 property, and others will outsource the property management function to a third-party firm. This is a matter of preference as well as a matter of asset class, as many sponsors that will outsource property management functions for more management-intensive asset classes (such as multifamily apartments and senior care) will do in-house property management on asset classes with fewer moving parts, such as long-term NNN lease properties.

To best sum up a DST sponsor's role, the DST sponsor is in the business of sourcing, financing, structuring and packaging properties to provide a pre-packaged 1031 exchange solution for 1031 investors.

Broker Dealers

The broker dealer is a securities company that is involved in the marketing and sales of DST 1031 offerings to investors. Broker dealers will often have a group of registered representatives that hold their securities licenses with the broker dealer. The broker dealer's role is to supervise their registered representatives and to provide support on securities-related matters.

The typical role of the broker dealer in a DST 1031 property is to analyze and provide due diligence on DST sponsor companies and their DST 1031 offerings. Broker dealers perform this function with either an in-house due diligence team or outsourcing due diligence work to third-party due diligence providers.

Upon the broker dealer determining that a particular DST 1031 property is appropriate for their registered representatives to offer to clients, the broker dealer will enter into and sign a selling agreement with the DST 1031 sponsor company. This in turn allows the broker dealer's registered representatives to offer to their clients the ability to invest in a particular DST 1031 property.

It is important to note that just because a broker dealer has conducted due diligence on a DST 1031 property (some actually conduct very little to no due diligence) and/or has outsourced due diligence to a third-party provider, this does not guarantee that a particular DST 1031 offerings is "safe." Due diligence does not guarantee profits, returns or safety of a particular offering. Investors should be aware that due diligence does not mean an offering will not have problems or issues and that even offerings with thorough due diligence conducted on them could result in an investor's loss of their entire principal amount invested. This is real estate, and there are no guarantees.

Registered Representatives

As noted earlier, the broker dealer will often hold the securities licenses of a group of registered representatives. The registered representatives are securities professionals who have successfully obtained certain securities licenses (e.g., Series 7, 22 and 63) to be able to offer to qualified investors the ability to purchase a 1031 DST property.

Many investors often ask if a real estate agent or broker is able to sell DST 1031 properties, and the answer is no. This is because DST 1031 properties are considered securities by federal and state regulators, as the investor is purchasing a piece of the real estate and not the whole property.

In the DST 1031 industry, we at Kay Properties and Investments have observed that there are two types of registered representatives who offer DST 1031 properties to their clients. The first type is what we call a specialist. This is a registered representative who specifically chooses to concentrate on DST 1031 properties for his or her clients. These registered representatives have helped many clients involved in 1031 exchanges and are often sought out by clients due to their reputation of specializing in these properties.

The specialist-registered representative typically is very active in the industry, attends industry conferences and has a strong understanding of commercial and investment real estate, as well as a strong understanding of the 1031 exchange and its rules and guidelines.

The specialist is often able to become a valuable resource to his or her clients and their CPAs and attorneys as the client is considering an investment in the DST 1031, because the specialist is involved in many, many DST 1031 property exchanges each and every year. At Kay Properties and Investments, we have grown a reputation throughout the industry and with our clients as specialists, and not generalists, because of the sheer amount of volume of DST 1031 business that we do each year and that we live and breathe DST 1031 properties every day.

The other types of registered representative that we have seen offer DST 1031 properties to investors are what we call generalists. The generalist is often a financial planner who has done one or two DST 1031 exchanges in his or her career. He or she may have the proper securities licenses to offer a DST 1031 property to clients; however, they often have a very rudimentary understanding of how these properties actually work and their potential benefits and risks.

The generalist often is preoccupied with all aspects of financial services, such as stocks, bonds, mutual funds, life insurance and annuities. Often the generalist will try to be all things to all people, and when a client has a 1031 exchange … the generalist is jumping right into DST 1031 mode for that client. The problem here is that these generalists often are not able to offer the valuable insight and experience, in my opinion, that a specialist may be able to. This is similar to how you would not want your knee surgery performed by a general practice doctor – you would want a specialist to potentially ensure the best outcome.

For a list of client testimonials and references of clients all over the United States that have chosen Kay Properties as their DST brokerage and advisory firm due to our specialized approach to DST properties please visit www.kpi1031.com/testimonials

Chapter 6:
Why Do 1031 Investors Choose DST Properties Over Traditional NNN Properties?

Chapter 6:
Why Do 1031 Investors Choose DST Properties Over Traditional NNN Properties?

Many clients that have been interested in doing a 1031 exchange into a NNN property find the DST 1031 property particularly attractive. These same clients often think that the only way for them to become passive owners of real estate is to purchase a NNN leased property; however, they often are very skeptical about placing such a large amount of their net worth into one single NNN property.

The DST 1031 option has become an increasingly popular option for investors that were previously considering a NNN property. Here are some of the reasons why 1031 investors may choose DST 1031 properties over traditional NNN properties:

Access to the same type of NNN leased real estate and tenants

Tenants such as CVS, BJ's Wholesale Club, Walgreens, Bridgestone/Firestone, Advanced Auto Parts, Sherwin Williams, FedEx, 7 Eleven, Starbucks and Dunkin' Donuts have been structured and used as DST 1031 properties in the past. Many investors love the idea of this caliber of tenants potentially paying them rent each month.

It is important to note that actual tenants will vary depending on the various DST 1031 properties available at the time of your exchange. The companies listed may not be represented in all programs and may not always be available.

Diversification

Many 1031 investors realize that placing a large portion of their net worth into a single NNN property is just not prudent. The idea of placing $2 million into a 7 Eleven, $1.8 million into a Starbucks or $4-15 million into a Walgreens or CVS makes clients nervous from a concentration risk standpoint.

The DST 1031 property provides a potential solution to investors wanting NNN leased properties and national tenants but with the ability to build a diversified portfolio of them. This is in contrast to "betting the farm" on a single piece of NNN property.

This concept is similar to how, often times, investors do not place 100 percent of their retirement accounts into a single stock and instead purchase mutual funds or exchange traded funds (ETFs). This is because they do not want their retirement accounts to "live or die" off of the performance of a single stock.

It is important to note that diversification does not guarantee against losses or guarantee profits. Investors should speak with their CPAs and attorneys for guidance as to if a DST 1031 property investment is suitable for their particular situation prior to considering a 1031 exchange.

Inflation protection potential

The way that the U.S. government has been printing money and so cleverly titling it as quantitative easing causes many investors to believe that inflation is coming. The problem with most NNN leased properties is the flat to miniscule rental increases that will potentially cause values to suffer. For example, Walgreens and CVS often have leases with primary terms that are from 20-25 years. During this 20-25 year period, the rent that they pay to the landlord will stay the same for the duration of the lease. Inflation could potentially wreak havoc on a static income stream such as this.

DST 1031 properties allow 1031 investors access to asset classes that historically have shorter lease terms than most NNN properties, such as multifamily apartments and self-storage properties, without the burden of active management. Asset classes with shorter lease terms can potentially be attractive to investors because when the leases are reset, the tenants are theoretically paying a greater amount than the year before, allowing the landlord to pass along any potential inflationary pressures to his or her tenants.

DST 1031 properties are "pre-packaged" for 1031 investors to be able to close on immediately

For an investor in a 1031 time crunch, a DST property that has been pre-packaged can be a potential solution to a very real capital gains tax burden. The 45-day identification period of a 1031 exchange moves very quickly, and investors wanting to purchase a single NNN property have very real risks, such as financing not coming through, issues with third-party reports such as appraisals and environmental reports and sellers not disclosing material items in the property's lease, such as early termination clauses or co-tenancy clauses, which can change the economics of the previously agreed-upon purchase price.

Much can go wrong with trying to purchase a NNN property. The DST 1031 provides a solution to investors not wanting to be burdened with the closing risks, resulting in a potentially failed 1031 exchange of a NNN property.

For a free infographic on why investors choose DSTs over NNNs, go to kpi1031.com/register and sign up.

Chapter 7:
The Section 721 Exchange

Chapter 7:
The Section 721 Exchange

Most real estate investors are familiar with the IRC Section 1031 exchange and have most likely been closely involved with a 1031 exchange in one form or another. The Section 1031 exchange has become a popular way for sellers to dispose of appreciated real estate and to defer capital gains taxes and depreciation recapture taxes.
Many of these same real estate investors that have utilized the Section 1031 Exchange time and time again have not heard of another powerful tax deferral tool allowed by the tax code, which is the IRC Section 721 exchange. The Section 721 exchange is typically used by Real Estate Investment Trusts (REITs) to acquire real estate from sellers that often don't want to pay large capital gains taxes. (1)

Here's how it works: instead of selling a property and doing a 1031 exchange to defer taxes, the seller contributes his property to a REIT's Operating Partnership in exchange for Operating Partnership Units (the Operating Partnership is the entity through which all REITs typically acquire and own their properties). This is all done on a tax-deferred basis utilizing the IRC Section 721 exchange.

This transaction is referred to either as a 721 exchange or an UPREIT (Umbrella Partnership REIT). Now the seller in exchange for his property (which is considered by the IRS to be "like kind" property) has Operating Partnership Units, which are equivalent and can be converted to shares of the REIT, on a tax-deferred basis.

Along with tax deferral, other potential benefits include the ability to realize the economic benefits of the REIT's entire property portfolio (including distributions of potential monthly operating income, potential capital appreciation and property diversification), liquidity options by partial conversion of OP Units to REIT shares (he can "peel" off what he needs to and pay the taxes on just that amount), the ability to fully divide his OP Units for estate planning among his heirs and, lastly, the ability to provide his heirs with a step up in tax basis, just as he would have been able to with his individual property.

The main caveat to the Section 721 exchange is that once an investor proceeds with the exchange, he loses the ability to continue 1031 exchanging and deferring taxes. He now only has the option to convert his Operating Partnership Units to REIT shares and pay his capital gains tax. Therefore investors who are in the midst of estate planning and who know that, upon their passing, their heirs will receive a step up in tax basis, which will eliminate the capital gains tax, often will consider the Section 721 exchange.

Other potential risks can include, but are not limited to, the REIT's management team making poor decisions (which could possibly cause properties to perform poorly and values to decline) and exposure to stock market volatility if the REIT they exchange into is publicly traded on a stock market.

Again, many investors have never heard of a Section 721 exchange because REITs typically will only acquire properties of institutional quality. This often leaves most investors out of reach of the 721 exchange and typically keeps it available to only institutional sellers.

However, I have seen the IRC Section 721 exchange made available to smaller investors through two distinct models. First is where a large REIT removes one of its institutional quality buildings from its portfolio and makes it available for individual investors to do a 1031 exchange into and hold title to it as a beneficial interest in a Delaware Statutory Trust (DST) or as a Tenant in Common (TIC) owner. The REIT, however, leaves a two- to eight-year call option on this building with the intent of "calling" it back into their Operating Partnership whereby the investors each contribute their DST interests in the building to the REIT's Operating Partnership in exchange for Operating Partnership Units on a tax-deferred basis, utilizing the IRC Section 721 exchange. (2)

The second model is whereby an investor is able to present his property to the REIT for evaluation. The REIT will not automatically accept the owner's property unless it has deemed the owner's selling value is reasonable, after which the seller will contribute his property to the REIT's Operating Partnership in exchange for Operating Partnership Units on a tax-deferred basis, utilizing the IRC Section 721 exchange.

Both of these models are used by REITs as a way to raise capital for their investment trusts. The resulting situation is potentially beneficial for both parties: the REIT has now raised a substantial amount of capital with one transaction, and the investor now has diversified his portfolio from one property to potentially hundreds (depending on the size of the REIT) on a tax-deferred basis.

The Section 721 exchange has been titled by Real Estate Weekly as "one of real estate's best-kept secrets."(3) Many investors have unlocked this previously "for institutions only" tax deferral strategy using one of the two models above. I believe that as the word gets out, the Section 721 exchange will become an increasingly popular tool amongst real estate investors to accomplish tax deferral, estate planning and diversification objectives, although it is unlikely that it will become as widely used as the 1031 exchange.

Please remember that both the IRC Section 1031 and Section 721 are complex tax codes; therefore an investor should consult his or her tax and/or legal professionals before making any investment decisions. This is not an offer to purchase securitized real estate, DST properties, REITS or any other securities. Such offers are made solely through the Private Placement Memorandum (PPM) or other appropriate offering document, such as a prospectus. Because investors' situations and objectives vary, this material is not intended to indicate suitability for any particular investment.

There are material risks associated with investing in real estate and DST properties, which are covered in Chapter 3.

(1) The Wall Street Journal, "Investors Broaden Reach with 1031-721 Exchange." May 5, 2004.

(2) Dividend Capital Exchange – Tax-Deferred Real Estate

Exchanges, September 22nd, 2008.

(3) Real Estate Weekly, "The benefits of selling property through an UPREIT." April 9, 2003.

Chapter 8:
The DST as a Cash Investment Vehicle

Chapter 8:
The DST as a Cash Investment Vehicle

Many of our clients have purchased DST properties as purely discretionary cash investments, even though they are not in a 1031 exchange. The reasons why investors will do this are many. Two of the main reasons that we will see are:

1) Clients that have exchanged with us into DST 1031 properties over the years will purchase DST properties as a cash investment due to wanting to continue to diversify out of the stock/bond markets as well as wanting to derive a tax-advantaged potential income stream.

2) Some clients will purchase DST properties via cash as a test run for 1031 exchanges in future. These clients like the idea of the DST 1031 but have not actually sold their buildings yet, so to help them build comfort with the DST 1031 they will make a cash investment prior to actually doing a large 1031 exchange.

If you would like a list of DST properties available for accredited cash investors, please visit kpi1031.com and register for free access.

Chapter 9: Kay Properties and Investments – A DST Brokerage and Advisory Firm

Chapter 9: Kay Properties and Investments – A DST Brokerage and Advisory Firm

At Kay Properties and Investments, we have chosen to be specialists, not generalists, in the DST 1031 industry. All we do, all day, every day is focus on DST 1031 properties and helping our clients. I founded my company to provide solutions to clients in 1031 exchanges and to be a specialized resource for investors.

We are headquartered in Palos Verdes, California (Los Angeles) and are licensed in all 50 states. We have clients located throughout the country, and many of them are CPAs, attorneys, real estate developers, high net worth families, rental and multifamily apartment owners, commercial property owners, land owners and institutions.

In 2013, we helped our clients purchase over $35 million of DST 1031 properties. In 2014, we helped our clients purchase over $50 million of DST 1031 properties. We are specialists, and I am an active DST investor personally.

Closing

I hope that you have enjoyed this book and have found it a valuable resource in your journey to learn more about DST 1031 properties. Please always feel free to reach out to me via email at dwightkay@kpi1031.com if you have any questions or needs. I wish you all the best in your journey!

Appendix A:
Client Testimonials

Appendix A:
Client Testimonials

At Kay Properties and Investments we have clients all over the country. Many of our clients were referrals from satisfied clients who realized their friends and family could potentially benefit by working with us, as well. We also have clients who are themselves Certified Public Accountants and attorneys throughout the country whom we have helped with their personal and family 1031 exchanges into DST properties. From there, those CPAs and attorneys continue to refer their clients to us, as well.

These testimonials may not be representative of the experience of other clients. Past performance does not guarantee or indicate the likelihood of future results. These clients were not compensated for their testimonials. Please speak with your attorney and CPA before considering an investment.

It was a pleasure working with Dwight Kay and his company this past year on my 1031 DST exchange. Everything has worked as Mr. Kay said it would, and the checks arrive at the same time each month. As I do more 1031 exchanges in the future, I look forward to working with Dwight Kay and Kay Properties with a DST to defer my taxes on the sale.

Richard V., Hotel Developer and 1031 DST Investor – Overland Park, KS

Thanks for following up so quickly on this... Your attention to customer service has reached far beyond my expectations, and I sincerely thank you for your diligence and patience. This is exactly how you win customer loyalty.

Tom U. – Madison, WI

Dwight,
Retirement has been great so far. The income generated from the DST's I purchased with your help has allowed me total freedom to pursue my passions and pleasures. My wife and I have just returned from a one-week vacation to the Turks and Caicos which I provided for my whole family, a total of nine people including children, their spouses and grand children. Had it not been for the tax-free exchange, my net worth and income would have been substantially reduced by federal, state and AMT taxes. So, thanks again and stay in touch. I expect more than one of the DST's will roll over in my lifetime.

Bill I. – Park Ridge, IL

Dwight Kay and Kay Properties & Investments provided a flawless execution of my 1031 exchange investment. Their process was quick and easy, and provided a great alternative to a single property investment. I highly recommend working with Dwight if you are considering a

1031 exchange.

Harry D. – Akron, OH

Dwight has been an amazing source of expertise and knowledge with respect to Delaware Statutory Trusts. He has treated all of my clients with special care, always ensuring that the most appropriate properties were suggested. During every step of the 1031 process, Dwight has been attentive and available to serve my clients. Dwight is an expert in his field and is a pleasure to work with.

David T., New York Tax Attorney

You are a model of expertise and responsiveness in your business. It was a real pleasure working with you.
All the best,

Dick S. – 1031 DST Investor – Chappaqua, NY

Just a short note to express thanks for helping us select the best 1031 replacement property. We were pleased with the help you offered on the paperwork. I wish our other investments were handled with the same attention to detail. Again, thank you for finding the best match for our needs.

Ken & Margie C. – 1031 DST Investors – Charlotte, NC

Just a short note to thank you for your work in getting me the detailed information I needed to make what I believe to be the correct 1031 investment decision.

Alex P. – 1031 DST Investor living in Europe

Dwight Kay is professional and highly knowledgeable. Dwight patiently educated and guided me to an informed decision leading to an easy, smooth, and successful 1031 Exchange DST purchase. Dwight will be my "go to pro" for all my future exchanges.

Rob L. – 1031 DST Investor – Chicago, IL

Dwight has been instrumental in helping me reach my financial goals. I have been an active real estate investor for years and was ready to turn from being an active investor to a passive investor so I could focus on other opportunities and interests. I am happy to say I made an investment with Dwight. …I would encourage any investor to speak with Dwight regarding their investments. He has been amazing for me, and I am so thankful to have done business with him.

Casey D. – Self-storage property owner and 1031 DST investor – Atlanta, GA

You did a fine job…

L.G. – 1031 DST Investor – Montana

Dwight, Thank you and I look forward to working with you (again). This was a smooth transaction. Happy Thanksgiving to you and your family.

John Y. – 1031 DST Investor – Englewood, FL

Dwight has shown a strong knowledge of how 1031 tax-deferred exchanges work and has been instrumental in helping us complete a number of transactions.

We have found Dwight thoughtful, knowledgeable, forward thinking, and dedicated to us as clients.

We are currently working with Dwight on a large 1031 exchange and look forward to completing this transaction with him in November.

We feel comfortable working with Dwight and recommend him to anyone that is need to investment advice.

Sincerely,

Barry Y. – 1031 DST Investor – Orange County, CA

Dwight, the four 1031 exchanges that you put together for me are performing well. You did an excellent job in your selection. I was especially impressed with your immediate responses to the many questions I had and for your assistance with the decisions that were required in my rather long process.

Thank you for your professionalism, and my best wishes to you for your continued success.

Bob W. – 1031 DST Investor – Nevada City, CA

We are writing this letter to recommend Dwight Kay and his firm Kay Properties. Dwight did an excellent job finding the right properties to 1031 exchange into for us. He was always available and prompt to answer our questions or concerns, which was as important to us as the actual investment (one exception, he was at a soccer game with his kids on a Saturday and asked if he could call me on Monday). His research and homework on the investment vehicles he proposed for us were spot on and met all of our criteria. When the smoke cleared he was also there to make sure we were satisfied with the whole process, along with working with our facilitator/exchanger. We have no reservations recommending Dwight to commercial real estate investors. We will certainly use him in the future.

Howard F. – 1031 DST Investor – Bonsall, CA

Hi Dwight,
It is our pleasure to provide our testimonial. You have been very professional throughout the whole process. In another word, you have been very patient and thorough with our questions and your guidance. We did not know the process at all in the beginning. Without your guidance, I imagine it would have been a difficult process for us.
Sincerely,

Jim and Ann M. – 1031 DST Investors – Foster City, CA

I would like to thank Dwight Kay of Kay Properties & Investments, LLC for steering us through our first 1031 exchange in California. We had done several previous exchanges in Maryland, but none with the personal touch that Dwight provided. He came out to our house, helped run through the figures to determine whether a 1031 made sense in this case, suggested several options for exchange properties, explained the benefits and risks of each, put us in touch with an excellent third party to handle the transaction, promptly returned calls to answer any remaining questions we had as the exchange progressed, and all in all made this a seamless process from beginning to end. We look forward to working with Dwight on any future exchanges we do.

Maurice and Janette L. – 1031 DST Investors – Torrance, CA

Thanks for all your help. You made this seamless.

Debby U., 1031 Exchange Investor – Orange County, CA

Dwight, it was a pleasure working with you during our 1031 exchange. Thank you for your expert guidance and your never-ending dedication to ensuring we were comfortable during every step of the process. Your goal for us was that we selected the potentially safest properties with the most reliable track records consistent with the best potential for future growth. We, Jan and I, are very pleased with the professional help you provided. Thanks again, a pleasure knowing you.

Larry D., 1031 Exchange Investor – Riverside, CA

Dwight Kay was not only highly informative and passionate in his work, but he made the whole process… an easy process. I feel his suggestions for properties to be solid and to be specific to what I was after. I will have no problem to use Dwight again in my future investment needs.

Lloyd F., 1031 Exchange Investor – Phoenix, AZ

What I like about Dwight is that he knows how to explain hard-to-understand financial concepts. He seems to like to teach his clients and uses excellent analogies to do this very effectively. I would recommend Dwight because in addition to removing the veil of complexity associated with 1031's, he is friendly, professional and prompt.

Sabina T. – 1031 Exchange Investor – West Hartford, CT

Greetings - it was a pleasure to work with Dwight. He was very informative about his properties and presented them with earnestness and enthusiasm but without the Hard Sell. Also when I needed help and information to complete my taxes concerning the properties, he was very prompt and helpful. If I do any such transactions again, he will be the one I call.

Jean L. – US 1031 Exchange Investor living in Thailand

Dwight was a critical element in my successfully completing my 1031 exchange. He gave me suggestions, guidance, did research for me and answered all of my questions. When the time comes to roll any of my properties over, I will go to him again.

Sergei P., Rental Property Owner and 1031 Exchange Investor – South Florida

---

I wanted to thank you for all the help you have supplied in solving my 1031 exchange questions and problems. Dwight not only supplied excellent 1031 investments but contacted the companies involved and had their representatives meet me while I viewed the properties at their locations. I have been highly impressed with Dwight Kay and the companies he is involved with in completing my 1031 exchange.

Greg U., 1031 Exchange Investor and Property Owner –
Brea, CA

Dwight Kay has been my broker for the past several years.
He is very knowledgeable about the properties he
recommends. He is very diligent, and when you ask a
question he always either answers right away or does
whatever it takes to find out and get back to you. Dwight
has the highest moral standards of any real estate broker
that I have ever been associated with. I have been a real
estate investor over the past 40 years and I would
completely recommend Dwight for any of your investment
real estate needs.

Dennis D., Multifamily and Commercial Property Owner –
Huntington Beach, CA

I have used Dwight as my real estate investment advisor
and have been very pleased with his depth of knowledge
related to real estate investment opportunities and his
dedicated, personable, and prompt attention to the needs of
his clients. Having invested in real estate for over 14 years,
I find Dwight to be by far the best person to assist in
finding high quality investment opportunities. I would not
hesitate to recommend Dwight to anyone who asks.

Fred M. - Huntington Beach, CA

Having sold our rental house in the Bay Area up north, we
found it uneasy to replace it with another in Southern
California. Thanks to Dwight's excellent guidance and
assistance, now we own multiple newer real estate
properties in ten states (vs. one single older house) –

diversified investment, with tax-deferred capital gains! Our 1031 Exchange via KPI was accomplished easily within 45 days. We've been most pleased with the work Dwight has done for us, particularly with his impressively pleasant diligence, responsiveness, communication and professionalism. Dwight is very honest and trustworthy... We are harvesting steady monthly direct deposit streams without having to manage anything.

David and Susie M. – Hacienda Heights, CA

Thank you for everything. I was surprised and delighted when the gift box appeared yesterday. An unexpected bonus!

When my TIC investment reached the end of its run this year, I was in a quandary as to what to do. I had a low basis going in, so an outright sale would be ruinous for capital gains taxes, but I was reluctant to commit to a sole owner real estate venture. My management skills are rusty, and I wasn't keen on the time and expertise needed. The TIC structure is going away - due to most lenders unwillingness to participate in them. The DST offerings through Kay Properties proved to be the ideal solution. I was very glad for the opportunity to diversify my investments both geographically and among different property types.

But your help in getting through the 1031 process and completing my acquisition into the three DSTs made all of this possible. From my viewpoint, the process was smooth, efficient, and very timely. This was due to your attention, diligence, and hard work. Many thanks!

I think I've got everything nailed down for now...

Distributions have already started - I can scarcely believe it! I will definitely consider Kay Properties in the future, and

would extend my enthusiastic recommendation.
Best regards,

Norm R. – Springfield, OR

For a full list of currently available DST 1031 properties, register today at www.kpi1031.com/register

Appendix B:
Press Releases

Appendix B:
Press Releases

Brooklyn, NY - Kay Properties and Investments, LLC Helps a Brooklyn, NY 1031 Exchange Client Purchase DST Properties.

Kay Properties and Investments, on behalf of a Brooklyn, NY client, has completed another successful 1031 exchange into DST properties. The client was looking for a way to successfully defer his capital gains taxes via a 1031 exchange in a timely manner and selected Kay Properties as his DST brokerage and advisory firm.

Dwight Kay, CEO AND Founder, commented, "With the client nearing his 45-day identification period, he was looking for properties that he could close on quickly that had no 1031 exchange closing risk. Since the DST properties had long term financing that was already locked and in place the client was able to identify and close on them in a very short timeframe."

Kay Properties & Investments, LLC is a DST brokerage and advisory firm providing DST 1031 exchange replacement properties to accredited investors. Registered Representatives at Kay Properties and Investments, LLC are licensed in all 50 states and have clients located throughout the country. For more information or to view our current property list please visit http://www.kpi1031.com.

Orange County, Florida - Kay Properties and Investments, LLC Helps Another CPA Client Purchase 1031 Exchange Delaware Statutory Trust (DST) Properties.

Kay Properties and Investments has helped another client purchase DST 1031 properties. The client being a CPA opted to work with Kay Properties as he was wanting an advisor that truly specialized in DST properties.

Dwight Kay, CEO and Founder of Kay Properties, commented, "Over the years we have helped multiple CPAs with their clients that were involved in 1031 exchanges, however, it is always an even greater compliment when the CPA himself chooses Kay Properties to help with his personal family 1031 exchange. We have helped clients all over the country successfully complete exchanges into DST properties with a number of those clients themselves being CPAs and Attorneys."

Chay Lapin, Vice President of Kay Properties, commented, "Not only was this client a CPA but he also held the Certified Financial Planner (CFP) designation which makes his selection of Kay Properties as his trusted DST property advisory firm an even greater compliment."

Kay Properties & Investments, LLC is a DST brokerage

and advisory firm providing DST 1031 exchange replacement properties to accredited investors. Registered Representatives at Kay Properties and Investments, LLC are licensed in all 50 states and have clients located throughout the country. For more information or to view our current property list please visit http://www.kpi1031.com.

Honolulu County, Hawaii - Kay Properties and Investments, LLC Helps Hawaiian 1031 Exchange Investor Close On a Portfolio of Delaware Statutory Trust (DST) 1031 Properties.

Kay Properties and Investments, LLC has successfully helped another 1031 exchange investor close on a portfolio of DST 1031 replacement properties. The client, a Hawaii based real estate investor, had recently sold rental property in downtown Waikiki and was looking for to do a tax deferred exchange into income producing properties that he would not have to actively manage.

Dwight Kay, CEO and Founder of Kay Properties, commented, "The client told us that he soon realized that nobody that he could find in Hawaii truly specialized in DST properties and he wanted a firm that could ultimately provide him with the expertise and guidance in DST properties that he was looking for, which ultimately led to him finding and deciding to work with Kay Properties."

Dwight Kay continued, "At Kay Properties, we are 100% focused on DST 1031 properties which is why many people opt to invest with us as opposed to our competitors. It is similar to how if you required knee surgery you likely could have your general practice physician perform the surgery, however you obviously would opt for a surgeon whereby all he or she does is knee surgeries day in and day out."

Chay Lapin, Vice President at Kay Properties, commented, "We are licensed in all 50 states to help our clients purchase DST 1031 properties and this Hawaii-based client is a very typical scenario whereby an out of state client will seek us out to help them with specified guidance and direction in the purchase of DST properties."

Kay Properties & Investments, LLC is a DST brokerage and advisory firm providing DST 1031 exchange replacement properties to accredited investors. Registered Representatives at Kay Properties and Investments, LLC are licensed in all 50 states and have clients located throughout the country. For more information or to view our current property list please visit http://www.kpi1031.com.

Monmouth County, New Jersey - Kay Properties and Investments Helps a New Jersey Real Estate Developer Successfully Complete a 1031 Exchange Into DST 1031 Properties.

Kay Properties and Investments was able to help a New Jersey real estate developer client successfully complete a 1031 exchange into multifamily apartment DST properties.

Dwight Kay, CEO and Founder, commented, "The client was looking for multifamily DST replacement properties that were in areas of the country with projections for potential increased population and job growth and ultimately selected the Southeast as the home for his 1031 equity."

Kay continued, "We often see clients from the Northeast and West Coast seeking to redeploy equity into areas of the country that are projected to potentially have strong amounts of job and population growth such as the Southeast and Texas."

Kay Properties & Investments, LLC is a DST brokerage and advisory firm providing DST 1031 exchange replacement properties to accredited investors. Registered Representatives at Kay Properties and Investments, LLC are licensed in all 50 states and have clients located throughout the country. For more information or to view our current property list please visit http://www.kpi1031.com.

Dane County, Wisconsin - Chay Lapin, Vice President With Kay Properties and Investments, LLC Helps a Wisconsin Client Successfully Complete a 1031 Exchange Into DST Medical Office Properties.

The client had recently been a part of a Tenant in Common property that had sold at a profit. Deciding that he didn't want to pay his taxes upon the sale and that another 1031 exchange made more sense, the client opted to work with

Kay Properties due to their specialization in the DST 1031 exchange marketplace.

Chay Lapin commented, "The client had very specific debt replacement requirements needing to be achieved for his 1031 exchange. Ultimately, a portfolio of Medical Office DST properties was decided on as the replacement properties for this exchange."

Dwight Kay, CEO and Founder of Kay properties, added, "Chay has been an instrumental part of helping our clients understand their options when it comes to selecting DST 1031 exchange properties. His level of commitment and patience to his 1031 exchange clients is commensurate with his level of dedication to his teammates and country as a former Olympic athlete."

Kay Properties & Investments, LLC is a DST brokerage and advisory firm providing DST 1031 exchange replacement properties to accredited investors. Registered Representatives at Kay Properties and Investments, LLC are licensed in all 50 states and have clients located throughout the country. For more information or to view our current property list please visit http://www.kpi1031.com.

Palm Beach County, Florida - Kay Properties and Investments, LLC Helps Florida 1031 Exchange Investors Complete Exchange Into a Multifamily Delaware Statutory Trust (DST) Property.

The clients were nearing the end of their 45-day identification period and were looking for options to complete their 1031 exchange in a timely fashion.

The clients chose to select Kay Properties and Investments and were able to receive truly specialized DST 1031 property selection advice and guidance.

Dwight Kay, CEO and Founder of Kay Properties, commented, "These clients, although living across the country from our headquarters, opted to work with Kay Properties for their DST 1031 Exchange purchase due to the fact that we live and breathe the DST 1031 exchange process every day for our clients. Our daily pulse on the market allows us to provide a level of guidance and understanding to our clients looking to purchase DST 1031 properties that we have been told over and over by current clients, that our competitors, just are not able to do."

Chay Lapin, Vice President, added, "Helping our clients throughout the country successfully complete their 1031 exchanges is a privilege that we do not take lightly. Hearing the relief in the client's voice when we tell them that their exchange is completed is priceless. This is another example of an out of state 1031 client choosing Kay Properties as their trusted DST 1031 brokerage and advisory firm, as opposed to a local advisor that may have access to DST properties but doesn't specialize in them nor have the level of understanding that our clients are looking for."

Kay Properties & Investments, LLC is a DST brokerage and advisory firm providing DST 1031 exchange replacement properties to accredited investors. Registered

Representatives at Kay Properties and Investments, LLC are licensed in all 50 states and have clients located throughout the country. For more information or to view our current property list please visit http://www.kpi1031.com.

Baltimore County, Maryland - California based DST 1031 brokerage firm, Kay Properties and Investments, LLC, helps a Maryland Certified Public Accountant (CPA) client successfully complete a 1031 exchange into Delaware Statutory Trust (DST) properties.

Dwight Kay, Founder and CEO, and Chay Lapin, Vice President, of Kay Properties and Investments, LLC have helped a Maryland CPA complete his family's 1031 exchange into a portfolio of DST 1031 properties.

Dwight Kay commented, "The client had recently sold a medical office building and was looking for a management free 1031 exchange property as well as the ability to diversify his 1031 exchange equity, and therefore a portfolio of DST 1031 properties was a perfect match for his goals and objectives."

Chay Lapin continued, "The client opted to work with Kay Properties and Investments on his DST purchases due to our level of understanding and specialization in the DST 1031 exchange product. We specialize in DST 1031 properties, which is why our client, even though he is from Maryland and we are a California-based, opted to work with our team here at Kay Properties and Investments. We are licensed in all 50 states, thus allowing us to serve our national 1031 clients from coast to coast."

Dwight Kay closed with, "We are excited to have been able to help another client successfully complete his 1031 exchange into DST properties. Our growth has been staggering over the years with over $50,000,000 of DST transactions in 2014 alone and we are incredibly grateful. As 2015 moves forward, we are excited as we plan to open our New York office next month in an effort to continue to assist our East Coast 1031 exchange clients."

Kay Properties & Investments, LLC is a real estate wealth advisory and DST brokerage firm providing DST 1031 exchange replacement properties to accredited investors. Registered Representatives at Kay Properties and Investments, LLC are licensed in all 50 states and have clients located throughout the country. For more information or to view our current property list please visit http://www.kpi1031.com.

Appendix C:
Educational Video Media library

Appendix C:
Educational Video Media library

To access our free DST 1031 property educational video media library, go to kpi1031.com/media.

Our videos include:

- About Kay Properties and Investments, LLC

- What is a DST 1031 Property?

- Types of DST 1031 Properties Available

- Reasons 1031 Investors Choose to 1031 Exchange into DST Properties

- Why Investors Choose DST Properties Over Traditional NNN Properties

The information contained in these videos, including the numbers used, is general in nature, approximate and intended for educational purposes to illustrate the experience of the representatives in this area. There are risks involved in investing into DST 1031 properties, including loss of entire principal amount invested. Past performance is no guarantee of future results. Potential cash flows/returns/appreciation are not guaranteed and could be lower than anticipated. Please speak with your CPA and attorney prior to considering a DST investment.

24378313R00059

Made in the USA
Columbia, SC
23 August 2018